"Stephen Rowan's new book, *Parables of Calvary*, is a wonderful insight into the final words of Jesus as he dies on the cross. The author connects these powerful words with some of the significant parables Jesus used to preach the Good News. Rowan has the unique gift of not only connecting the Seven Last Words of Jesus with the parables, but he also connects them with the lives of men and women today. In clear and often poetic prose, he provides the reader with a rich resource for prayer and thoughtful reflection. It is well worth reading and rereading."

Most Rev. Thomas J. Murphy
Archbishop of Seattle

"In *The Parables of Calvary* Rowan guides the reader over territory that has been crossed many times through the Christian centuries: prayerful consideration of the seven last words of Jesus. He skillfully explores this holy ground, this inexhaustible source of meditation, pointing out new details, different angles from which to view the mystery of the cross and the words of Jesus. It is a commonplace in theology that the words and deeds of Jesus' ministry are the key to understanding the gospel crucifixion narratives. What I especially appreciate is the way Rowan applies this principle to specific texts. For each of the last words of Jesus, he also uses a passage from one of the parables, resulting in a weaving of many scriptural texts, all of them converging toward a prayerful listening. Read it slowly. And read it more than once."

Rev. Jeremy Driscoll, O.S.B., S.T.D.
Professor of Theology, Mount Angel Seminary, Oregon

"Father Rowan's beautiful reflections on the last words of Jesus help us understand the rich meaning of Jesus' entire life and ministry. The author's biblical scholarship, literary knowledge, deep spirituality, and pastoral sensitivity are all evident in *The Parables of Calvary*. This book will be very much appreciated by anyone who wants to enter more fully into the mystery of Jesus' life and death. It is a pleasure to read.

Rev. Lawrence T. Reilly, Th.D.
Pastor

"These seven reflections are not just for lenten meditation; they are words for all seasons. Stephen Rowan is a critical reader of the Scripture, a keen observer of the human heart, and a skilled weaver of words. He combines these gifts well in this tapestry of amazing grace. These hearty reflections are just the right length for a period of meditation. They are good examples of what can happen when we put the gospel stories into conversation with our own stories. When we hear Jesus forgive and set people free in his day, we realize that he is calling us to a new life of love, mutuality, and peace today.

"Fr. Rowan brings us within earshot of the cross so that we can hear the parables of Jesus echo through the last "words" of Jesus. In this way, we can hear more clearly words that affirm trust instead of betrayal, that call for community instead of division, and that evoke generosity and service instead of domination and violence."

Richard M. Gula, S.S.
Professor, St. Patrick's Seminary, Menlo Park, California

"Father Rowan has written an appealing series of brief but literate chapters on the seven last words of Christ. Each reflection relates an utterance of the dying Savior to the content of his life and mission. Although each meditation can be read independently, the collection as a whole gives a stimulating, rounded picture of the values that moved the Christ of the gospels."

Peter Chirico, S.S.

STEPHEN C. ROWAN

The PARABLES of CALVARY

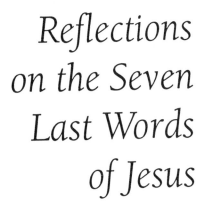

*Reflections
on the Seven
Last Words
of Jesus*

XXIII
TWENTY-THIRD PUBLICATIONS
Mystic, Connecticut 06355

With Gratitude
to
The Monks of Mt. Angel Abbey
St. Benedict, Oregon

PAX ET BONUM

Twenty-Third Publications
185 Willow Street
P.O. Box 180
Mystic, CT 06355
(203) 536-2611
800-321-0411

Library of Congress Catalog Card Number 93-61555
ISBN 0-89622-576-3
Printed in the U.S.A.

Contents

Introduction   1

CHAPTER ONE
The Power of Forgiveness   3
Parable: Matthew 18:12-13
Word: Luke 23:32-34

CHAPTER TWO
The Promise of Hope   9
Parable: Matthew 13:44-46
Word: Luke 23:35-43

CHAPTER THREE
The Potential of Love   15
Parable: Luke 10:25-37
Word: John 19:16-27

CHAPTER FOUR
The Endurance of Faith   21
Parable: Luke 20:9-18
Word: Matthew 27:45-47, Mark 15:33-36

CHAPTER FIVE
The Longing for Truth
Parable: Luke 15:8–9
Word: John 19:28–29

29

CHAPTER SIX
The Burden of Acceptance
Parable: Mark 4:3–9
Word: John 19:30–37

35

CHAPTER SEVEN
The Triumph of Trust
Parable: Luke 15:11–32
Word: Luke 23:44–56

41

Afterword

47

Introduction

Like the parables, which were his favorite way of teaching, the words of Jesus from the cross are short but surprising. Understood to the full, they are even unsettling. They were spoken out of a whirlwind of human misery, and they address everyone who witnesses misery like the cross in our own time. With power they reveal the worst that human ignorance and evil can do, and at the same time they reveal the forgiveness of God which reaches beyond death to life.

Two kinds of listeners will hear the teaching of Jesus: To the indifferent or hostile, the words are nonsense; to the faithful, they reveal the mysterious workings of God's rule: the graceful call to discipleship; the cost of it; the price of ignoring the call, and the joy of heeding it. Both in the life of Jesus and on the cross, it is as the old man Simeon said it would be: When Jesus speaks and acts, the thoughts of many hearts are revealed (Lk 2:33–34).

It is the purpose of the following reflections to pause over the words of Jesus, to consider them in the context of the gospel from which they are taken, and to make the connection between their teaching and the teaching of the parables. One parable more than others receives special emphasis in these reflections: the parable of the lost son and the prodigal father from Luke 15.

When Rembrandt painted the parable's climactic moment of reunion, he showed the hands of the father embracing his son while the son, with his back to the spectator, presses his head firmly against the father's bosom. On the faces of both is serene peace and joy, while the place where they stand radiates the surrounding darkness with light.

The genius and the skill of the artist have expressed in this image the power of the parable's teaching that God reaches out to the human soul even when it has placed itself at a distance, and then the hands of God warmly embrace the soul who trusts that God wants not exile but homecoming.

This message of enduring love speaks clearly through the words of the cross. It is a message not only of comfort but also of challenge. Those who take courage from these words learn as well that they must pattern their lives on the way of forgiving love if they are to find the life of Christ.

The seven reflections that follow may be read over a period of several days or at one sitting. In either case, they should be read in the context of the gospels. For that reason, at the start of each chapter a portion of one of Jesus' parables is highlighted as well as one of the words that he spoke from the cross.

Through Jesus' words, may the thoughts of your heart be revealed to you, and may you hear there God's message of enduring love.

CHAPTER ONE

The Power of Forgiveness

If a shepherd has a hundred sheep and one of them is lost, won't he leave the ninety-nine and go in search of the lost one? And if he finds it he will rejoice over it more than the ninety-nine who never strayed.

—Mt 18:12–13

 **WORD FROM THE CROSS**

Father, forgive them (Lk 23:32–34).

The hill of calvary is the last mountainside that Jesus climbed in order to teach, and the tree of the cross was the last place from which he taught. The seven words that Jesus spoke from that place speak to us as directly as they spoke to all of the people gathered around the cross so many years ago. As we listen to the words from the cross, we hear the four gospels from which they are taken summed up, each with its own emphasis, its ringing challenge, and its graceful comfort.

Taken altogether, the words of Jesus speak to the human heart about what concerns us deeply: our need for unwavering acceptance and our need for purpose. These concerns of the heart are touched only slightly by the promises of politicians or by the glib and glossy images of the ad writers. But the heart hungers for a word that speaks unwavering love to us. We wait for the word that calls out from the deep silent mystery who is God and proclaims that God is seeking us relentlessly even if we have not as eagerly been seeking God. We yearn for the God who knows our worth and our purpose and who tells them to us and then challenges us to become what we are.

The words from the cross are deceptively short and even commonplace. Like the stories that Jesus loved to tell—called parables—the words from the cross seem smooth and simply clear, and yet all the while they contain great depths of meaning. They can erupt at any time with extraordinary power, even as they seem to speak of ordinary things.

Jesus taught in parables because he wanted to catch the attention and then gain the commitment of the people who heard him. Everyone likes to hear a good story, and most people will try to work out the point of a story if it grabs their interest and if they have the time to think it over.

But Jesus also told parables because he was facing a collection of hard-headed and powerful enemies—the rulers of the people—who wanted people to think that the way things were was the way things always had to be. The parables challenge this way of thinking surely but quietly. They show in the very course of the story that ordinary life can in fact erupt at any time into something new and unexpected: a harvest that yields a hundredfold (Mk 4:3–9), an invitation to come up higher (Lk 14:7–11), forgiveness of debts (Mt 18:23–35), a treasure beyond price hidden right under a person's feet (Mt 13:44). The words from the cross—so like the parables in their simple language—are in fact surprising offers of grace here and now.

On the hill of calvary, Jesus faced the same kinds of people he faced all during his public life, and so in his first word from the cross he startled the crowd—as he always did—to think otherwise about what they were doing, to reconsider the sense of their actions. Jesus hinted in his first word from the cross that even if everyone agrees that something must be so, something else might in fact be the case. Jesus prayed "Father, forgive them..." and with this word he overturned the Roman version of history and the ignorance—not to mention the cowardice—of anyone who agrees with it.

Throughout his public life, Jesus spoke with authority about the rule of God before whom every authority on earth falls short. With God's rule as the standard of human conduct, there is no end to the need for conversion or reform, because there is never enough justice or truth or peace in the world. And because he held out to people the challenge of God's standard for them, Jesus became in the eyes of Rome an enemy of Caesar. To Jerusalem he became an enemy of the people because he invited trouble for them from their Roman rulers. According to the high priest, Caiaphas, Jesus had to die, lest the whole nation perish. For Caiaphas, life was supposed to continue as it always had, with no surprises, no deviation from ancient laws and interpretations, with no amazing grace.

With Jesus executed, the call to God's rule and to another way of life would be crucified, dead, and buried. Rome and Jerusalem could then try to establish the official version of history, that Jesus was of no account, that there is no higher appeal for truth and justice in this life than the pragmatic arrangements of the power brokers. But even as they prepared the cross for Jesus in order to cancel him out, Jesus cried out his version of events above the sounds of hammer and nails. His prayer, "Father forgive them," meant that the "establishments" of Rome and Jerusalem were wrong to crucify him and that he was innocent.

Many people, maybe even most of us, would like to trust that the institutions we have designed with human ingenuity will serve all of our needs just fine. If we just lower our sights to more modest goals, keep our noses to the grindstone, and try not to make too many waves or to hope for too much, everything will work out for us in the end. To those who think this way, the prophet is merely a dreamer and certainly an inconvenience. But Jesus challenges this attitude and calls it ignorance, not enlightened thinking. He prays, "Father forgive them, they do not know what they are doing."

In the crucifixion of Jesus all of human history comes into sharp focus: the all-too-human attempt to betray the dream, to drive it out, and to kill it. At the same time, at the center of the storm, the crucifixion focuses on our call to see what we are doing *for what it is* and to do otherwise. When we are forgiven, we can move beyond what we have done and take the chance to begin again.

This first word from the cross is like so many of the parables that Jesus told in which the lost is found and people are given a new chance through forgiveness. A woman finds a lost coin, a man finds a lost sheep, and perhaps the most beloved story of all, a father finds one lost son and urges his surly brother not to stand outside but to join in the celebration (Lk 15).

When Jesus told these stories he was trying to defend himself against those who accused him of welcoming sinners and eating with them. Jesus upset people by his familiarity with sinners because they could not see that he was going beyond the law to do what the law required, which was to re-establish for people their right relationship with God. Jesus was offering the company of God to people who never dreamed that they qualified for it. They had never kept the law as a kind of proof for qualifying. To these Jesus announced the good news: God accepts you for who you are at any time. All you have to do is recognize yourselves for who you are in God's eyes and act in such a way that you are true to yourselves.

No wonder, then, that Jesus was driven out as an enemy of good order. He was crucified so that life as usual could go on over his tomb. But the word from the cross is "Father, forgive them," and with that word all people who hope for a better life can take courage. With that word Jesus becomes the center of a new version of history, one in which the rule of God becomes the measure of human actions and the forgiveness of God becomes the reason to hope that new life is possible.

St. John tells us that near the place where Jesus was crucified there was a garden, and in that garden a tomb. After Jesus was taken down from the cross and buried in that tomb he rose again to show that through him we can get the garden back: We can join ourselves in spirit to the obedience of the new Adam and become with him hearers and keepers of the word. Through him we can come to know our human worth and purpose. The words "Father forgive them" rebuke the shortsightedness of human thinking, reveal the unwavering love of God, and touch our hearts with hope.

Prayer

L ord Jesus, with outstretched arms you reveal the wideness of God's mercy. Even in the midst of moral darkness you show the way to life through enduring love.

Give us faith to accept your judgment of our sin and to accept with thanksgiving your offer of forgiveness. Amen.

CHAPTER TWO

The Promise of Hope

The Kingdom of heaven is like treasure hidden in a field, which someone finds and hides; then with great joy the person goes and sells everything and buys that field.

—Mt 13:44–46

† WORD FROM THE CROSS

Today you will be with me in Paradise (Lk 23:35–43).

Nailed to the cross over the head of Jesus was an inscription that read: "Jesus of Nazareth, King of the Jews." The indictment was written by Pontius Pilate, the Roman governor, and it was meant to degrade not only Jesus but the entire Jewish people who were subject to Rome. It was as if Pilate were saying with lordly contempt: This wandering teacher from Galilee, this troublemaker, this crucified criminal is your king.

In John's gospel, the leaders of the people object to the inscription and complain that Pilate should have written that Jesus only claimed to be king. But Pilate, seeing the discomfort and probably enjoying his moment of victory, replies with what sounds very much like the non-explanation of an official announcement: "What I have written, I have written."

The other gospel writers recorded no such protest. Instead, the leaders of the people seemed so eager to share in the governor's power that they ignored the insult to themselves. Taking their cue from the inscription, they degraded Jesus even further. Like jackals who crowd around the carcass only after the lion has made the kill, the rulers of the people circled the cross and shouted their insults. They scorned Jesus for his lack of power: "He saved others," they cried out, "let him save himself if he is the Christ, the chosen one!" It was a scene of howling rejection and scorn, a scene of moral chaos and of bleak despair.

Adding to the moral confusion is the fact that Pilate had Jesus crucified between two thieves—as if he were one of them, maybe even the chief or the worst of them. Like the suffering servant of Isaiah's prophecy, a grave was assigned for Jesus among the wicked and a burial place with evildoers (53:9).

But now we are about to learn something interesting about human psychology in the face of seemingly hopeless odds. Two men made two entirely different choices in the face of despair.

According to Luke, one of the thieves, embittered by what was happening to him, believing that he was far from deliverance of any kind, and brought to despair by the taunts of the crowd, joined in the hellish scene of scorn and contempt. "Are you not the Christ," he cried out, "then save yourself—and us." These are the words of someone who no longer has any hope but who is trying, perhaps, to be just a little less alone by making his contempt at least the same as everyone else's.

It is terrifying to hear what despair will make someone think or say. This man thought of himself as someone at the end of the road, like a cornered rat, with no way of retracing his steps and with no desire, it seems, to begin again. He saw himself as lost, but if he had his freedom back he would only have used it to find his way to the same place again. This thief turned sour at even the idea of hope. He accepted the Roman version of history and joined in the verdict of the mob. To him, Jesus was a failed dreamer, one more reason not to trust anyone except himself.

The voice of this despairing thief is heard often in our own time. It comes not so much from those who are down and out, but even more loudly from those who are well off for the moment, those who are considered the financial and intellectual elite. These people enjoy positions of influence. They set the standards of fashion in dress and in ideas, but they know how arbitrary their standards are and with what little conviction they believe whatever they believe. They suspect that one day they will fall from influence while others whose attitude is just like theirs will rise. This is the rut or cycle of life. It is not fair, just a fact.

So much of the sadness of people in our time can be traced to this implicit despair, that nothing they think or do really matters. The despair is concealed under a round of frantic activities. People steal a moment of diversion here and there, they steal some tangible good now and then in order to distract themselves from what they believe is the nothing that their lives amount to. The American writer Thoreau claimed that most people lead lives of quiet desperation, and he added that even their amusements are desperate; they need to escape from themselves, but they cannot find anything worthwhile to which they can give themselves. These thoughts are echoed in the words of the thief who taunted Jesus with the cry, "If you are the Christ, then save yourself—and us!"

This is one attitude toward seemingly hopeless odds, but there is another. The good thief, as we call him, saw on the face of Jesus the calm assurance of someone whose thoughts are somewhere just ahead of him and who knows that he is on his way to completing a mission. The good thief saw power in the face of Christ because Jesus absorbed the insults of the crowd and was not shaken by them.

And the good thief saw in Jesus the joy that comes from completing the work that was given him to do. The eyes of a thief are trained to be quick and piercing; they are skilled at detecting where treasure can be found. To the good thief, Jesus looked for all the world as if he could lead the way out of the hellish despair that hemmed him in on every side.

And so he took hope from the good that he saw and asked for a share in whatever Jesus had to give. "Jesus, remember me," he prayed, "when you enter your kingdom." And in his answer to the thief, Jesus made clear more exactly what it was that he had to give. Jesus offered paradise, a kingdom stripped of its military and material meanings, which is in fact a garden. That is what "paradise" means, a garden where fully human growth takes place. Jesus offered this thief the chance to find life even on the cross. He told him, "I assure you, this day you will be with me in paradise."

The difference between hope and despair is simply trust that Jesus is right and that the crowd is wrong. Although it may seem otherwise, faith is convinced by the cross that the wisdom of God is wiser than human wisdom and that the weakness of God is stronger than human strength.

Jesus taught that the kingdom of God is like treasure buried in a field or like a merchant's search for fine pearls (Mt 13:44–46). The field that holds the treasure may not look like much, but the one who has found the treasure knows that it is there and no matter what the neighbors say about how foolish it is to pay the price, that person gives everything to buy the field. And a merchant who knows what pearls are worth cares not for the size or the number of what he is buying. He cares only for the quality, and so he sells everything he owns to buy the pearl of great price.

The good thief trusted that he had found in Christ the treasure that he had sought in other ways all of his life. And so he had hope that even on the cross he would find a way to more life: "Jesus, remember me when you come into your kingdom." And Jesus, like the good shepherd he is, having found the one sheep that was lost, put him on his shoulders rejoicing and carried him home (Lk 15:3–7). With love he said to the thief and to all who hope as he does, "This day, I promise you, you will be with me in paradise."

Prayer

You give us hope, Lord Jesus, by giving us your love. Even when we are discouraged by loss and frightened by the evidence of evil, paradise cannot be far away when you are with us.

Give us strength in moments of moral confusion to put our trust in you, the shepherd and guardian of our souls. Amen.

CHAPTER THREE

The Potential of Love

But a Samaritan while traveling came near him, and when he saw him, he was moved with pity. He went to him and bandaged his wounds and put him on his own animal. Then he took him to an inn and cared for him.

—Lk 10:25–37

 **WORD FROM THE CROSS**

Woman behold your Son (Jn 19:16–27).

According to St. Luke, as Jesus was on his way to Jerusalem, and only a short time before his crucifixion, he told a story about a man who fell into the hands of robbers. The man was beaten, stripped, and left for dead (Lk 10:25–37). His own people—his fellow Jews—left him lying in the road as they passed by. A priest and a levite, the very pillars of the nation, walked by on the other side of the road, and so they widened the distance between themselves and the other. They were well off, he was not; they were at the top of society, the traveler was on the bottom; they were in, and he was out.

The man lay wounded and alone until a stranger came by, a foreigner in fact—a Samaritan. He dressed the man's wounds, lifted him up, put him on his own donkey, and took him to a place where he could be cared for. This story of the good Samaritan is one of the most famous Jesus ever told, and he told it because a lawyer had asked him to answer a tricky question: "And who is my neighbor?" In other words, if love of God and neighbor fulfills the law, how can I fulfill that law? Just exactly who is my neighbor? Once he heard Jesus' story, the lawyer knew that there was no hard and fast definition that could be applied in the abstract. Instead, he had a practical standard to apply: "The one who did good to the man, that one is the neighbor."

We have heard this story so many times that we may not catch the full surprise of it: "Who is my neighbor? The one who *does* what is neighborly." The story warns us not to trust in labels or in names only. "Priest" and "Levite," it turns out, mean nothing to the wounded Jew; only "Samaritan" does, and until that moment of love *in deed*, the Samaritan was a stranger and even an enemy. This is surprising perhaps, but true, and Jesus himself lived by the lesson of this story.

Once someone in the crowd raised her voice to praise the womb that bore him and the breasts that nursed him; someone with kind intentions, no doubt, tried to praise Jesus by praising his mother. But he replied, "Rather, blessed are those who hear the word of God and keep it." In other words, if his mother deserved praise, and she did, it was not because of the relationship that biology gave her, but because of her faith. Bearing him and nursing him created a certain kind of relatedness, yes, but the greater affinity is one of loving trust and service. At another time, when someone told him that his mother and his family were looking for him, Jesus stretched out his hands to the crowd and said, "Here is my mother and brothers and sisters. Those who do the will of my Father in heaven are mother and brother and sister to me."

The teaching of Jesus calls into question the usual social distinctions we make among ourselves. It calls for the creating of a new society based on shared trust in him, a shared willingness to join him in doing the will of his father.

The wounded Jew by the side of the road has no "neighbor" in those who were otherwise close to him, the priest and the levite; instead, his neighbor is the one who does good to him, the Samaritan stranger. In the same way, Jesus on the cross is like that wounded man; he is left to die alone while people pass him by or keep their distance. He is rejected, thrown out of the city and crucified, disowned precisely so that the powers that be can show their power and increase their power by destroying him.

On the cross we see revealed how hateful to the world and how thoroughly rejected is the teaching and the person of Christ. And yet in the midst of that dark and clamorous scene of rejection, we learn, according to John, that there stood by the cross of Jesus his mother and, with his mother, the disciple whom he loved. They said nothing, but they showed their relationship to him by where they stood. And as they stood, they waited for word—like the true disciples that they were.

At the foot of the cross they formed a small and tight circle of resistance to the howling mob. They strengthened each other by their mutual witness; they served Jesus by their steadfast attention to him. This is what it means to be church: not just taking the name Christian, not just writing position papers or keeping rituals, but rather being a brave "communion of the faithful."

As we read the signs of our times, we find that it is becoming both more difficult and more easy to be church today. It is more difficult because the church enjoys no obvious support, as it once did, from intellectuals and politicians. In fact, today the church is more likely to be a subject of ridicule or suspicion from those quarters. And in the face of such ridicule, it is harder to witness and to minister.

And yet, for these very reasons it is also easier to be church today. There is now a clear place to stand over against a culture that is in many ways ego-centered, skeptical, and narrowly pragmatic. It may not be comfortable, but the place to stand is with the woman and the disciple who witness to Jesus as the word of life.

The "word" that mother and disciple heard from Jesus strengthened their communion, so that they were united more strongly to one another through him. "Woman," said Jesus, "behold your son; son, behold your mother."

Woman and disciple were revealed to one another by a word that meant not only "look" but even more "look and *see*," see what you mean to one another. "Behold," see more deeply into the community that you share because you are standing together by the cross. And through this communion with one another you have hope that where you stand is the place to be. You reduce somewhat the anxiety that arises from feeling too much alone in your witness to the Word who is truth and life. The woman and the beloved disciple showed us in their neighborly care for the wounded Christ the love and the courage that it takes to be the servant church.

The faith of the woman reversed the faithlessness of her counterpart Eve, and by her faithful and loving witness to the Word who is Jesus, she brought him to birth in the world. The beloved disciple who was called "son" was born again through the word mediated by the woman.

"Woman behold your son; son behold your mother." Those who stand by the cross of Christ are brought close to him and to one another by their mutual witness in the midst of a harsh and unbelieving world. They prove themselves to be disciples by where they stand, and where they stand makes possible a real communion of the faithful, the very picture of what it means to be church today. On the hill of calvary their witness and communion of love shine out like light in the darkness, and it is a light that with God's help will not be overcome.

Prayer

T o all who gather in your name, Lord Jesus, you have given the gift of church. You nourish us with your word and with the sacraments that flow like water and blood from your side, and you reveal the love that redeems us.

Give us wisdom to understand the mystery of the cross and give us courage to witness it in the world. Amen.

CHAPTER FOUR

The Endurance of Faith

Then the owner of the vineyard said, "What shall I do? I will send my beloved son; perhaps they will respect him." But when the tenants saw him, they threw him out of the vineyard and killed him.

—Lk 20:9–18

✝ WORD FROM THE CROSS

My God, my God, why have you forsaken me? (Mt 27:45–47, Mk 15:33–36).

In his story "The Death of Ivan Illych," Leo Tolstoy describes how Ivan feels as he lies on his deathbed wracked with cancer while his wife, who is in full health, comes to visit him: "Ivan Illych looks at her," Tolstoy writes, "scans her all over, and sets down against her her whiteness and plumpness, and the cleanness of her hands and neck, and the glossiness of her hair, and the gleam full of life in her eyes. With all the force of his soul he hates her...Her attitude to him and his illness is still the same."

Tolstoy was a shrewd observer of human psychology. A person in pain, removed for a time from the ordinary course of life, soon feels the loneliness and even the resentment of watching from the sidelines while others continue the daily routines. To the sick, the healthy seem to be busy about many things, with thoughts and plans of their own that do not include them. Being at some distance from life as usual, the sick and especially the dying can regard those who are well with envy, and even in some cases with resentment. The pain of the sick or dying person lies deep and gnaws quietly at the soul; it draws the person into it and forces attention onto itself, whereas a healthy person feels no such pain and seems to be living at the surface of things, with no depth.

The encounter of Ivan and his wife is painful precisely because it is so true to life. But beyond the pain that divides the ill from the healthy there is an even more fearsome pain. It is the kind that Jesus suffered on the cross, the pain of feeling cut off and abandoned by God. It was as if Jesus was living out in the flesh the absurd situation he described in one of his own parables. It is the story of a man sent to a distant place by his father, a person of importance, to collect rent on his properties (Lk 20:9–18). The son took up the mission, convinced of its importance and eager to please his father, but when he arrived he found that the tenants had no intention of paying rent. To prove the point, they had been beating the rent collectors previously sent by his father. Finally they showed their complete contempt by seizing the son and killing him. It is very likely that the son felt cheated and abandoned, even absurd, for having been sent on such a fool's errand.

According to Luke, Jesus told a similar version of this story while he was on his way to Jerusalem, and in that story he was no doubt revealing something of the turmoil in his own soul, a turmoil that was to hit him with full force on the cross. Jesus, who said that he had come to do the will of the one who sent him, clearly saw that he had a mission to complete, but at some point he must have wondered if the whole mission had not been a cruel mistake. He was baffled, caught on the one hand between trust in the one who sent him and on the other by the apparent failure of what he had come to do. And so he cried out in real anguish the first words of Psalm 22, "My God, my God, why have you abandoned me?"

Humanly speaking, Jesus was in the position of all who have ever found themselves without purpose, with no sense that their lives can make a difference or even mean anything. Like Ivan

Illych, Jesus wondered out loud, "It cannot be that life has been so senseless, so loathsome...there's something wrong."

This dull despair was also put into painful words by the Jesuit poet Gerard Manley Hopkins whose personal struggles gave him a feel for this desperate state of the soul. He wrote:

I wake and feel the fell of dark, not day.
What hours, O what black hours we have spent
This night! what sights you, heart, saw; ways you went!
And more must, in yet longer light's delay.
With witness I speak this. But where I say
Hours I mean years, mean life. And my lament
Is cries countless, cries like dead letters sent
To dearest him that lives alas! away.
I am gall, I am heartburn. God's most deep decree
Bitter would have me taste: my taste was me;
Bones built in me, flesh filled, blood brimmed the curse.
Selfyeast of spirit a dull dough sours. I see
The lost are like this, and their scourge to be
As I am mine, their sweating selves; but worse.

As Hopkins says, the abandoned state is the state of lost souls; and to say that Jesus descended into hell is to say for one thing that Jesus knew the human condition to its full extent. He was not acting human, he *was* human, truly God and truly human, and his cry from the cross plumbed the depth of just how much our humanity can suffer.

We see that suffering today in the starved faces of the hungry in Somalia and Ethiopia, in the frightened faces of refugees from Haiti, in the terror-stricken faces of beleaguered citizens of Bosnia.

Closer to home, we see suffering in those who come every day to the doors of our churches looking for food, for shelter, and just as much for company. We have visited friends dying of cancer or of AIDS, and we have held their hands to comfort them as they move ahead into the dark.

Only within the past year, we learned with shock and sorrow of five missionary sisters caught in the merciless crossfire of Liberia's civil war. Not so long ago, several Jesuit university professors and their housekeeper and her daughter were dragged from their sleep and killed in El Salvador. And several years before that, four women missionaries were murdered in El Salvador. To many, the mission of these witnesses to the gospel may seem fruitless. Their deaths may seem absurd.

Jesus knew suffering like this. On the cross he shared the place of the lost son in another of his parables, who according to the story, found himself alone in a distant land, out of resources, pinched by famine, and with no one willing to give him shelter (Lk 15:11–32). Of course, it was the son's loose living that brought him to this condition, whereas Jesus was innocent of any wrongdoing. And yet, innocent as he was, Jesus shared the son's condition. He knew what it was like to feel forsaken. And precisely because of his innocence, Jesus had even more reason to cry out, "My God, my God, why have you abandoned me?"

It is only because he took all of our suffering humanity upon himself that Jesus was able to take all of it with him out of despair and onto the road back to life. We know that in the parable the son moved beyond deep despair to the point where he resolved to put one foot in front of the other and take the road back home. He had no idea of the reception he would get. He just trusted that there would be a place for him once he arrived.

And the words of Psalm 22, which Jesus cries out from the cross, also end with the conviction that God has not despised the poverty of the poor; God has not turned away but has listened to the cry for help. We are never told how the psalmist made this turn-around from despair to confidence or why the son in the parable ever resolved to go home again. Instead, we are invited to wonder how it is that at its darkest point darkness touches day; how it is that at some point west becomes east; how it is that the seed that falls into the ground dies, but then becomes a rich harvest.

The cross reminds those who see it with faith that God can accomplish good from anything that happens to us—even the cross. From the human point of view, there is the lifting up of our hands onto the cross in witness and total trust. From God's side there is the lifting up of the witness into glory. There is the rewarding of the one who witnesses faithfully in the world to gospel truth. The despair, the anxiety, the suffering are all brutally real, but just as real is the homecoming that takes place through the cross. What looks like the end of the story becomes instead the turning point.

Once the despair that clouds the vision lifts even for a moment, we can see in the light of faith that the mission's purpose has been accomplished: God who wants sin to be seen for what it is, shows it fully on the cross; God who offers forgiveness to the worst of sin offers it above all on the cross. And God who wants people to come to life through forgiveness, shows them the way out of their despair through the cross.

Lifted up from the earth on the hill of Calvary, the cross bridges the gap between heaven and earth. Through the cross God joins us in our suffering and invites us to come home in faith through Christ.

Prayer (Psalm 130)

Out of the depths I cry to you, O Lord.
Lord hear my voice!
Let your ears be attentive
to my voice in supplications!

I trust in you, Lord; my soul trusts in your word.

My soul waits for you, Lord,
more than sentinels wait for the dawn....

For with you, Lord, is kindness and plenteous redemption. Amen.

CHAPTER FIVE

The Longing for Truth

What woman having ten silver coins, if she loses one of them, does not light a lamp, sweep the house, and search carefully until she finds it? When she has found it, she calls together her friends and neighbors and rejoices.

—Lk 15:8–9

 **WORD FROM THE CROSS**

I thirst (Jn 19:28–29).

Jesus cried out "I thirst," knowing that all was now fulfilled and in order to "fulfill the scriptures completely." Physical thirst is one of the painful sufferings of crucifixion; it is one more way that in his humanity Jesus comes close to us in all that we can suffer. And yet the thirst of Jesus is also a sign of something more. That is why it is sad to hear the response of the soldiers to this word. Perhaps they meant well, but they misunderstood what Jesus was saying. When he cried out "I thirst" in order to fulfill the scriptures, they brought him sour wine to satisfy his physical thirst. Clearly they did not know what they were doing. What are we to think that Jesus meant by this word?

Readers of the gospel of John will remember another time that Jesus was thirsty; it was at the same hour as his crucifixion—the noon hour—and he had come in his journey to a well in Samaria where he sat down, weary from his travels, and asked a woman of Samaria for a drink of water (Jn 4).

As they talked, Jesus led the woman into a discussion, not of the water standing at the bottom of the well, but rather of living water that flows upward into eternal life, water that is in fact the gift of God. When Jesus says he is thirsty, he surely has in mind not only physical drink to quench his parched mouth, but also a life-giving drink for his spirit.

The scriptures of the Jewish people speak of running water in many ways that point out its meaning in more than physical terms. The psalms, for example, recall that during the exodus from Egypt "God cleft rocks in the wilderness and gave [the people] drink abundantly as from the deep. He made streams come out of the rock and caused water to flow down like rivers." Water in the desert is a picture of God's mercy; the relief from physical thirst is a sign of relief from abandonment and death. The lost people found their way to life through God's care for them even in the desert. And it is perhaps because of that key moment in their history that in another psalm the people praised God as the good shepherd who leads his flock to green pastures beside restful waters that restore the soul.

Water is a sign of the life that is found when God and the human person are at one. Just as we cannot live without water, just as we need water even to *be* ourselves, so, too, we need to know and to love God. To be at one with God in this way is to be nourished at the source of what is truth and love. And so the psalmist prays from the heart: "Like the deer that yearns for running streams, so my soul is yearning for you, my God. My soul thirsts for God, for the living God, when shall I come and behold the face of God?"

When Jesus says "I thirst" he sums up the hope for God that runs through all of the scriptures. Stripped naked and thirsting on the cross, he reveals once and for all that even in the absence of every good we can see and touch, there remains the choice of waiting for God.

It is like searching for a lost coin until it is found—and then rejoicing (Lk 15:8–9); or persisting for justice—as the widow did before the judge (Lk 18:1–5) until it is received.

The cross contradicts everything we take to be solid reality and shows every tangible good we know to be only partial and temporary. Far from reflecting our everyday values, the cross is a scandal and a stumbling block because it puts into question everything we rely on to secure happiness for ourselves. On the cross, Jesus was deprived of every good thing: of food and drink, of his good name, of his freedom to move about, even of the comfort of a human hand placed into his own to comfort him. The cross does not mirror back to us the good life as we think it to be, and so it forces us to ask which is more real: the way we stake our claims to happiness on tangible goods or the thirst of the crucified Christ for God alone?

The cross is surely not a mirror of what we call "the good life"; instead, it is a window into what we need to desire if we are ever to find real life. That is why the cross is called our atonement: It is the way we can see beyond our everyday preoccupations in order to learn how to be at one with God, the giver of every good thing.

With the words "I thirst" Jesus shows that feeling abandoned is only one part of the story; the next part begins with waiting for God who is like "quenching water" to the one who is thirsty for it. God is "faithful love" to the human person who cannot live without it. But, as St. John has told us, the sign of the cross is often misunderstood (when it is not ignored or rejected as absurd). The thirst of Jesus for something more than physical water is understood in the end only by faith. Only a few people have had the power to describe that "something more," that peace for which the faithful soul is yearning. One such person is the poet Hopkins. He knew all too well the depths of despair that come from knowing only the self, but he was also granted by way of compensation, it seems, the peace of knowing God. He said that it is like the longing for a haven—this longing for heaven—and he imagined the feeling to be like that of a woman who was choosing Christ by taking the veil as a nun. Putting himself in her place, he wrote:

I have desired to go
Where springs not fail,
    To fields where flies no sharp and sided hail
And a few lilies blow.
    And I have asked to be
Where no storms come,
    Where the green swell is in the havens dumb,
And out of the swing of the sea.

The thirst of the faithful soul for Christ is like the thirst of Christ himself on the cross: a longing for the water and the springs that do not fail, a longing for the truth and the love that last.

Prayer

In your hunger and thirst to do the will of the one who sent you, Lord Jesus, you show us the way to life in this world. When life seems sterile and hopeless, there remains even in the desert of our exile God's call to life that flows like water from the rock.

Give us a hunger and a thirst like yours so that we, too, will seek the life-giving nourishment of God's love and truth—which never fail. Amen.

CHAPTER SIX

The Burden of Acceptance

A sower went out to sow...and some seed fell on the path and the birds ate it. Other seed fell among thorns and was choked out.... Other seed fell into good soil and brought forth grain, growing up and increasing and yielding thirty, sixty and a hundredfold.

—Mk 4:3–9

✝ WORD FROM THE CROSS

It is finished (Jn 19:30–37).

he words of Jesus in the gospel of John are majestic and packed with meaning. They are majestic because they are the words of the one sent by God, the only-begotten son, full of grace and truth. And even one word from Jesus is packed with many meanings all of which hint at the depth of the wisdom he reveals. We are warned to look for that wisdom even when it comes to us in an everyday guise. The word was made flesh with all the human needs and limitations of the flesh, so that with faith we could know the glory of God.

According to John, the last word Jesus spoke is only one word in the Greek: "Tetelestai" (in English "It is finished"). This one word has two meanings, both of which convey a sense of triumph.

First, "It is finished" means that the work is done, the mission is complete. The one sent can now return to the one who sent him. The second meaning builds on the first: The work is finished not only because it is brought to a close, but also because it is brought to perfection, brought to the end for which it was taken up in the first place.

What is the work that Jesus came to do? According to John, it was to drink the cup, to take from the Father's hands the life-in-death that was handed to him. Having come from God, Jesus thirsted to drink the cup. His work was to return to God while at the same time revealing to us that this journey from God to God is also the way that our lives can be full of grace and truth.

To do the will of the one who sent him—every day and in every circumstance—this was meat and drink to Jesus. It shaped his life until it was over and until it reached its goal, until, that is, it was finished.

On the cross, Jesus showed us for the last time the pattern of our salvation. He moved from feeling abandoned, to a decision to trust that God is faithful (even when God could not be seen), and finally to reaching for the cup and finding God in the doing of God's will.

John calls the crucifixion of Jesus a "lifting up" because it shows all at once the inseparable combination of two things: the lifting up of Jesus onto the cross (in other words his accepting of what he had to suffer in order to be a faithful witness of God in this world), and then the lifting up of Jesus in triumph (because in doing the will of the one who sent him he finds life and reveals that life to others). The cross is indeed a sign of contradiction. It cancels out the usual understanding of what counts for success in our time and shows us success in the most unlikely of places. We look for success perhaps in the polls or in the pages of glamour magazines; we envy the powerful and the glitterati who establish their status by flaunting the symbols of conspicuous consumption. We listen eagerly even to trivial words and we attach importance to them only because they are nationally televised or have earned so many millions of dollars in revenue.

The cross contradicts these symbols of success and importance and promises us life when we do as Jesus did, and that is when we do the will of the one who sent us. Responding to the words of the cross, taking them to heart, requires the same kind of faith needed to accept the lessons of the parables. In all of the parables of Jesus, an everyday, ordinary human experience reveals the rule of God. A merchant searches for fine pearls (Mt 13:45–46), a shepherd looks for a lost sheep (Lk 15:3–7), a farmer casts a wary eye on a barren fig tree (Lk 13:6–9), servants use or bury their talents (Mt 25:14–30), bridesmaids wait for a bridegroom (Mt 25:1–13). All of these are scenes from the everyday lives of the people with whom Jesus walked. Yet in his teaching Jesus challenged people to shake off their everyday, routine ways of looking at things, to see even in their own lives signs of the faith, hope, and love to which God was calling them. And once people caught a hint of that life, they knew well enough how much they needed to change. More and more they knew they needed to move away from the surface of life into the depths of it, where God can be found.

The parables show that the rule of God is of great worth; it is a mystery of grace and truth. At the same time, the rule of God is awesome because it exacts from us no less a price than the gift of ourselves. We cannot serve equally well both God and something less than God. The cross of Christ is the place where Jesus finished the work of this teaching in all of its mystery and awe.

St. John tells us that after Jesus says "It is finished," he hands over his spirit, and from his side flow out blood and water which signify a fountain of life for the woman and the beloved disciple.

Jesus is like the sower who sows the seed and who waits for the harvest that will come according to how receptive the soil has been (Mk 4:3–9). The soil cannot receive the seed if it is rocky and without depth, or full of thorns that choke the seed, or too far to the edge of the field. The soil must be receptive or the seed will never take root.

In the same way, the words from the cross went out to many kinds of people who were gathered on Calvary: to the jeering leaders of the people and to the indifferent soldiers who were casting dice for the clothes of a man they assumed to be a criminal. The words went out to the thieves who were crucified with Jesus, and as we have seen, to the woman and the disciple who stood by the cross. Today, the words go out to us as well, and only an honest searching of the heart will reveal just where we stand among all those people on Calvary.

It is St. John who tells us not only that the word goes out, but also what happens to it when it does. The word came into the world and the world did not recognize him; he came to his own people and his own did not receive him; but to those who did accept him he gave the power to become children of God... to become people whose lives share in the same grace and truth of "the word made flesh."

Prayer

 our word has taken root in us, Lord Jesus, or we would not be pondering even now the mystery of your self-giving on the cross.

Bring your word to full fruition in our lives. Finish the work you have begun in us. Help us to produce a harvest worthy of being gathered up into everlasting life. Amen.

CHAPTER SEVEN

The Triumph of Trust

But while he was a long way off, his father saw him and was filled with compassion; he ran and put his arms around him and kissed him.

—Lk 15:11–32

✝ WORD FROM THE CROSS

Father, into your hands I commit my spirit (Lk 23:44–56).

T he last words of Jesus according to Luke are taken from Psalm 35, the prayer of the Jewish people: "Father, into your hands I commit my spirit." And it is perfectly consistent with the picture of Jesus that Luke draws that Jesus should sum up his life with a prayer.

Luke's gospel often depicts Jesus at prayer: at his baptism, before he is transfigured on the mountaintop, and during his agony deep in the garden of Gethsemane. It was from prayer that Jesus learned what the Father had in mind for him, and it was because Jesus gained such confidence and strength from prayer that his disciples asked him to teach them how to pray. This, according to Luke, was how they learned the Lord's prayer: by asking Jesus what it was that he said to his Father when he was alone, and what it was that gave him such joy.

The last words from the cross are words of perfect trust: "Into your hands I commit my spirit." They speak of a surrender which is not a defeat, a homecoming that will prove to be a victory. Jesus had been cast out from the city, and like the scapegoat of the ancient ritual he had been despised and rejected so that life in Rome and Jerusalem could go on as usual. The leaders of the people wanted no more talking in parables about the rule of God. Instead, there would be edicts, meetings, and taxes; there would be small talk and business as usual, but there was to be no word of God.

This was the plan of the leaders, but the stone rejected by the builders would soon become the cornerstone of a new way of life, and so in these last words from the cross we hear not only trust but also joy in a victorious homecoming.

When Jesus prays "Father, into your hands I commit my spirit," he shows exactly how much he trusts the Father and for what reason he gives his trust. Strictly speaking, God has no hands, and so when he trusts himself into the Father's hands, Jesus trusts in something that is there but cannot be seen. He must move ahead into the dark with only trust that what he calls the hands of God will be there to uphold him.

What is it, then, that Jesus hopes will hold him fast? What could he mean by the hands of God? We will find our answer in the books of the bible revered by the Jewish people. The book of Genesis tells of God's making of creation for a purpose and especially of God's shaping the man and the woman into life and then placing them in the garden where they will be happy. The book of Exodus, too, recalls how God stretched out his hand to deliver his people from Egypt under the leadership of Moses and then stretched out his hand to drown their enemies. And the prophet Isaiah, speaking to the Jewish people many years later while they were in exile, tells them to have courage because God who gave shape to the first creation will shape for them a new creation, a return from exile, and God will raise up a new deliverer for them, even in the unlikely person of the pagan ruler Cyrus.

Above all, the psalms speak of God's care for all creation and especially for the chosen people. To the psalmist we are all the work of God's hands; God's hands have made and fashioned us (119:73), and more than that, in God's hands are the depths of the earth; the heights of the mountains are God's, and the sea also—that ancient symbol of chaos—the sea is God's, for God's hands made it and also formed the dry land (95:4–5).

To speak of God's hands, then, is a way of speaking about God's purpose for us and of God's kindness toward humanity, which we experience even in everyday life. The scriptures regard this world as a creation formed by God's hands, not a chaos. It has shown itself at wonderful and terrible moments to work by laws that are guided by wisdom. This is why the psalmist can pray with great trust: "Though I walk in the midst of trouble, you [God] preserve my life. You stretch out your hand against the wrath of my enemies, and your right hand delivers me. The Lord's purpose will be fulfilled for me; your steadfast love, O Lord, endures forever. Do not forsake the work of your hands."

Jesus trusts that God will be faithful. He trusts that God who has promised life will deliver life despite the worst that his enemies can do. Even if his friends suppose in their despair that this must be the end of the story, Jesus trusts that it is not.

The cross is a sign of hope, thanks to the words of Jesus. He invites us to see it that way. The cross, both in its shape and in its function for us, is like the anchor of a ship that is thrown ahead into the harbor and then grounds the ship and keeps it steady in the storm. The cross takes hold in the silent mystery who is God and keeps us steady in our trust that the ground of our being is gracious and will not give way, let the storm rage as it will.

To look at it another way, the cross stands midway between heaven and earth; it is lifted up on the hill of Calvary for all to see, precisely so that it can mediate between the human question and the divine response, between our sometimes confused lives and the clear invitation to come home through repentance and love.

On the cross our many sins are revealed in the tortured Christ, and at the same time, God's grace is revealed in the outstretched hands of forgiveness. Once again we see on the cross the enacting of the parable of the lost son (Lk 15:11–32). When the prodigal son is feeding pigs in a foreign land, he recognizes his desperate state and resolves to take the road home. He rehearses a speech to his father in which he recounts the wrong he has done and then he dwells on how unworthy he is to be called a son. The speech sounds almost too well rehearsed, and the son sounds far too untrusting of how his father will receive him.

But once he is ready, he sets out on his way and only then do we find out—to our surprise—that the father has been coming to the hill every day looking for his son, watching with hope for his return. And upon seeing his son the father does not wait for him but runs to him and with no words, with no sermons, with no rebukes, takes him into his arms.

This is the Father that Jesus trusted and told us about, and that is why he had the confidence to say "Father, into your hands I commit my spirit." If we have heard these words with faith, then we, too, can take hope and like the prodigal of the story come home to God with Christ through the cross.

Prayer

 ord Jesus, you have given us an example that we should follow in your footsteps. For the joy that was set before you, you endured the cross, disregarding the shamefulness of it, and you have taken your place in glory at God's right hand.

Through the mystery of your death and resurrection, you show us the way home from exile to fullness of life. Lift up our hearts with hope and keep us strong in faith and love along every step of our life's journey. Amen.

Afterword

T he words from the cross—like the parables of Jesus—speak to us from out of the silent mystery who is God. Like the flashing of a star across the heavens, the words of Jesus emerge from the depths of God's wisdom and then return to it, shedding light on our path but also revealing how much more there is to God than we will ever understand.

This revealing word touches the heart of our deepest concerns for purpose and hope. We know that we cannot provide that purpose for ourselves out of our own wishful thinking. Only the thing itself, a purpose that is revealed, not manufactured, has the power to save.

It is especially when we know ourselves to be tossed on a sea of difficulties and doubts that the words of Jesus prove to be, in the words of Shakespeare, like "a star to every wandering bark whose worth's unknown although its height be taken."

Like the polestar to a ship at sea, the words of Jesus stand firm as a point of reference. In the words of John Paul II, Jesus is the stable reminder of the mission of love that God has given to each person in this world. With the unwavering reference point of the star or of the word for guidance, the ship and the human soul can avoid shipwreck and find their destined harbor.

We find more in the words of Jesus than merely self-survival;

we also find community. Through the words of Jesus we find a whole company of others who are united in response to them. And it is through the company of other witnesses that we grow in the hope that the purpose revealed in Jesus is indeed as steady as it seems.

Reflecting with the church on the words of Jesus, both in the parables and from the cross, we can grow wiser about the ways of amazing grace and find a way of bringing it to light in our world.

Of Related Interest...

Words from the Cross
Stephen C. Rowan
Applies the timeless words of Jesus to the questions and needs of today. Lenten spiritual reading for all ages.

ISBN: 0-89622-354-x, 54 pp, $3.95

Nicene Creed
Poetic Words for a Prosaic World
Stephen C. Rowan
An ideal introduction to the Creed for catechumens and for teens preparing for confirmation. Questions for study and reflection included.

ISBN: 0-89622-451-1, 80 pp, $5.95

Still on the Cross
Meditations on the Human Condition and the Desperate Passion of Jesus
Loretta Girzaitis & Richard L. Wood
Links the passion of Christ with contemporary injustice and highlights the Christian mission to continue Christ's saving work.

ISBN: 0-89622-449-x, 80 pp, $5.95

The New Scripture Way of the Cross
Based on the Stations led by Pope John Paul II
Bill Huebsch
This booklet offers a form for meditations that uses the Passion of Our Lord based on the actual passages found in the New Testament.

ISBN: 0-89622-551-8, 32 pp, $.99

If They Could Speak
Ten Witnesses to the Passion of Jesus
John D. Powers
"Voices" from the past—James, Judas, Pilate, Mary Magadalene, and others—come into our time to reveal truths about Jesus.

ISBN: 0-89622-421-x, 64 pp, $4.95

Available at religious bookstores or from

TWENTY-THIRD PUBLICATIONS
P.O. Box 180 • Mystic, CT 06355
1-800-321-0411